Made for Each Other

Why Dogs and People Are Perfect Partners

Dorothy Hinshaw Patent

Photographs by **William Muñoz**

CROWN BOOKS FOR YOUNG READERS ♛ NEW YORK

To Jimmie Harrington and Marcin Radwan and their great
canines, Ryky and Dex, who knew how to share courage and love
—D.H.P.

To the memory of my mother, who always worked for libraries
and the books found there
—W.M.

Acknowledgments

With thanks to the following people for their help with this book: Dr. Gregory Berns, Lars Bjurström, Jasmine Bloemeke, Jayann Chipma, the Daniel family, Drew Estep, Emily Gray, Allison Herther, Dr. Ludwig Huber and his colleagues at the Messerli Research Institute in Vienna, Kate McDermott, Dr. Ádám Miklósi and his colleagues in the Family Dog Project in Budapest, Dr. Daniel Mills, Carol Thill, Renee Van Camp, and Victoria Werner.

Text copyright © 2018 by Dorothy Hinshaw Patent
Photographs copyright © 2018 by William Muñoz

Published in the United States by Crown Books for Young Readers, an imprint of Random House Children's Books, a division of Penguin Random House LLC, New York.

Crown and the colophon are registered trademarks of Penguin Random House LLC.

Visit us on the Web! randomhousekids.com

Educators and librarians, for a variety of teaching tools, visit us at RHTeachersLibrarians.com

Library of Congress Cataloging-in-Publication Data is available upon request.
ISBN 978-1-101-93104-2 (trade) — ISBN 978-1-101-93105-9 (lib. bdg.)
ISBN 978-1-101-93106-6 (ebook)

MANUFACTURED IN CHINA
10 9 8 7 6 5 4 3 2 1
First Edition

Contents

Part One:
A Perfect Partnership

Dogs and people, people and dogs—we've been buddies for thousands and thousands of years. How did this relationship start, and why do people and dogs love each other so much?

Ancient Bonds

Prehistoric wolves were the ancestors of all the dogs in the world. Genetic evidence suggests that this probably happened in two different areas: eastern Eurasia and western Eurasia. We'll never be sure just when people and wolves started living and working together, but the more we learn, the earlier we believe that time was. Scientists once thought wolves had become dogs just 12,000 or 13,000 years ago, not long before we domesticated animals like goats.

But now, by looking into the **DNA** of today's **dogs,** we can see **changes** in genes that might go back **100,000 years** or more!

Recently, scientists studying the DNA of a wolf fossil from Siberia concluded that dogs and wolves probably split at least 27,000 years ago and that dogs and wolves interbred for thousands of years after that.

This Saudi Arabian saluki, bred from ancient hunting dogs, looks like its ancestors—shown in rock art (left) created thousands of years ago in North Africa.

Becoming a Team

Perhaps our partnership started when wolves discovered the trash heaps of bones and other scraps from kills that people dumped outside their villages. Wolves that weren't afraid of people would have found food there without having to hunt. They would have had an easier time surviving and breeding, leading to pups that also felt comfortable around people. Maybe those ancient people put up with the garbage-eating wolves because they kept dangerous animals away and helped clean up their trash.

The **wolves** could also have been an **early-warning system** for the village—**howling** or **barking** when **strangers appeared.**

Bit by bit, these animals almost tamed themselves.

Homeless dogs today still survive on human garbage—much like some wolves may have done thousands of years ago.

Or maybe wolves and humans became hunting partners first. Thanks to their powerful sense of smell and ability to hear four times farther than humans, wolves could find prey easily. They could also run much faster than people to chase down their target. But humans, with their spears and other weapons, could kill large prey like mammoths more effectively than wolves could. So a human-wolf partnership would benefit all.

According to Nez Percé Indian elder Horace Axtell, his ancestors could recognize the special howl of wolves that announced they'd found prey. The Indians would be alerted and then kill the prey and share the remains with the wolves.

Wolves hunt in packs, which allows them to bring down large prey like elk and moose.

How to Become a Dog

In order to live around people, many things about wolves needed to change.

Wolves	Dogs
Fear humans	Bond with humans
Ignore human gestures	Understand human gestures
Don't care what humans think	Want humans' praise and affection
Are active during the day and at night	Are active during the day and sleep at night
Are aggressive to strange wolves	Are usually not aggressive to unfamiliar dogs
Rarely bark	Bark to communicate
Live to hunt and reproduce	Bred to do specific jobs for humans

Wolves and **dogs** have many **physical differences.**

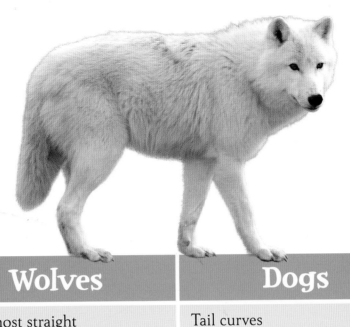

Wolves	Dogs
Tail almost straight	Tail curves
Ears point upward	Ears are often floppy
Color a mixture of black, brown, and gray, or pure black or white	Many different colors, including solid white, black, and many shades of brown; white with spots; and tricolor
Normal size ranges from 50 pounds to 130 pounds	Usual size ranges from 2 pounds to more than 250 pounds

A Special Doggy Talent

Dr. Brian Hare has brought attention to one important way in which dogs are special. From the time they are puppies, dogs quickly understand that when a person points, there could be a ball to fetch or a tasty morsel of food to eat. On the other hand, chimpanzees—the animals most closely related to us—have trouble grasping this simple idea: *If a person points to something, I should check it out.*

Dr. Brian Hare and his "lab partner"

What about wolves? If raised in captivity, they can learn to understand pointing, but it isn't easy for them. So dogs probably haven't inherited this skill from their wolf ancestors. It seems that dogs' thousands of years of living with humans have helped make this important ability come naturally. Understanding pointing opens up a whole world of learning for dogs.

Like children, **dogs** can **learn** the **names** of objects **easily.**

They can quickly find items like food or toys, partly because they instinctively know to pay attention when a person points something out.

Dimitri Belyaev
and his
friendly foxes

From Fearful to Friendly

How did the changes from wolf to dog happen? A Russian project might help answer this question. More than fifty years ago, scientist Dimitri Belyaev wanted to see if careful breeding could make silver foxes easier to handle. Raised for their beautiful fur, silver foxes are naturally afraid of people. Sometimes they bite, too.

Belyaev started mating the least shy foxes together. Within a few generations, the foxes became friendly toward people. Surprisingly, they also started to look different. Some had spotted coats. Others were white or black. Some had floppy ears or curved tails.

Friendlier foxes had pups that looked more doglike.

They also started behaving like dogs: barking, wagging their tails, and whimpering for attention. They even licked the experimenters.

Researcher Lyudmila Trut found that the friendlier foxes' blood had lower levels of certain stress hormones, which helps explain their lack of fear toward humans. Many scientists believe that "creating" dogs from the wild wolves was the same as or similar to what happened in breeding the foxes.

Dogs by Design

It probably didn't take long for people to start choosing which dogs to breed together to strengthen traits that were useful to humans. With dogs that were well suited to perform specific jobs, the human-dog partnership thrived. The American Kennel Club has sorted dogs into groups, based on their jobs:

Hound — Greyhound — Ibizan Hound — Beagle

Terrier — Airedale Terrier — Border Terrier — Bull Terrier

Toy — Pug — Miniature Pinscher — Papillon

Sporting — Cocker Spaniel — Golden Retriever — English Setter

Non-Sporting — Shiba Inu — English Bulldog — Dalmatian

Herding — Lowland Sheepdog — Shetland Sheepdog — Australian Shepherd

Working — Doberman Pinscher — Great Dane — Siberian Husky

Protecting Their Human Pack

Guarding comes naturally to dogs due to their wolf heritage. Each wolf pack has its own territory that it guards from other wolves. If a stranger enters a pack's territory, it risks death. Wolves are also very protective of their pups.

While their first guarding job for people probably involved watching over villages, selective breeding has developed dogs that carry out other protective roles.

Seen and Heard

Some scientists believe that humans couldn't have domesticated herd animals like sheep and goats without the help of dogs. Think about it—sheep can run fast on four legs, even over the steep, rough ground that is their natural habitat. There's no way a person or even a group of people could manage a herd of sheep alone. But with dogs, the job is much easier—the dogs do most of the work!

The herding instinct comes naturally to dogs, due to their wolf ancestors. Wolves get a herd of prey running and look for an

injured or slower animal. They cut that individual out of the herd and chase it down. People have bred dogs to work a herd the way wolves do. But instead of attacking the sheep, herding dogs stop short of biting.

Today, breeds like border collies are expert sheepherders. They move the flock based on the shepherd's commands. They will cut sheep from the flock and bring them to the shepherd. They can even find sheep that have wandered far away, out of sight, and bring them back home.

Hunt and Fetch

When a wolf pack hunts, it leaves the pups behind with their mother when they are still nursing, or with a "babysitter" wolf when they are older. The hunters bring back food to their hungry pups. Today dogs use these skills to help people hunt.

Pointers use their **sensitive noses** to **find** birds that **hide** in reeds and brush on the **ground,** such as **pheasants** and **grouse.**

When it finds birds, the dog freezes in a "point" position to alert the hunter.

At the hunter's signal, the dog charges the birds, and the hunter shoots them as they fly up.

The dog then finds the birds and brings them to the hunter.

Some dogs, like Labrador retrievers, specialize in water retrievals. These dogs happily give up prey in exchange for approval, affection, and the occasional treat.

Part Two:
The Science of Love

Our loving relationship with our furry friends is a fascinating subject for research. What's the science behind our close bond as friends, coworkers, and loyal companions?

Science explorers

What's on Your Dog's Mind?

Dr. Gregory Berns at Emory University believed that if we could look into a dog's brain, we could see if it works like ours. We use an MRI machine to find out how human minds work. Why not try it on dogs?

This seemed to be an impossible task. To get clear readings from an MRI,

Holding your head still takes a lot of practice!

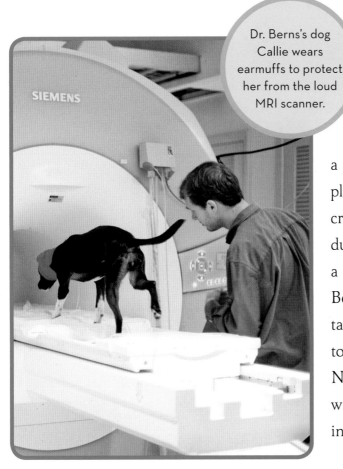

Dr. Berns's dog Callie wears earmuffs to protect her from the loud MRI scanner.

a person must stay completely still inside the cramped, noisy machine during the scan. Would a dog ever do that? Dr. Berns used patience and tasty bits of frankfurters to get dogs to cooperate. Now they just hop up and wriggle into position inside the machine!

Dr. Berns's scans of his canine crew show that when a dog thinks about food or sees or smells a member of its human family, its brain lights up in a reward center called the caudate nucleus, which also helps produce loving and joyous feelings in humans. No wonder dogs wag and dance and kiss when they see us.

We call it **love** in **people**–can we call it **love** in **dogs,** too?

The Loving Touch

Doesn't it feel good to pet a dog, especially one with soft, silky fur? Well, you're not the only one who feels good—so does the dog! Petting a dog increases helpful hormones in both your blood and the dog's, including oxytocin, which helps you feel relaxed, lowers your blood pressure, and slows your heart rate. Petting a dog also lowers the level of a hormone named cortisol, which is triggered by stress. These effects are so strong that people who have dogs are much more likely to survive a heart attack than those who don't.

You don't even
have to **pet** your **dog**
to feel **better**—just
look into his **eyes.**

Merely sharing a gaze can increase oxytocin in you and your dog.
As researcher Brian Hare says, it's as if your dog is "hugging you" with
his eyes!

Face to Face with a Dog

Our faces can reveal our feelings—even when we try to hide them. Scientists in the lab of Professor Ludwig Huber in Austria are finding that dogs can tell the difference between happy and angry human faces. The dogs were shown either the top or bottom halves of a pair of faces. Some dogs got a reward for choosing the happy face, while others were rewarded for picking the angry one. The dogs could tell the difference even when shown new faces. Not only that, but choosing a happy face seemed less stressful to the dogs than having to select the

In Dr. Huber's lab, Beautiful rests her head as she looks toward a screen with images on it. The camera can detect how her eyes move in response to the images.

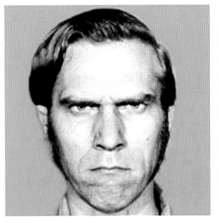

These are some of the images Dr. Mills showed the dogs, with human faces that are angry, neutral, or happy.

image of an angry face. "It seems that dogs dislike approaching angry faces," Dr. Huber explains.

British scientist Dr. Daniel Mills is also studying how dogs react to human faces. Dogs can tell the difference between happy and angry human faces, but when they see a "neutral" (neither happy nor angry) human face, they find it unsettling. Dr. Mills believes this might be because dogs always interpret human faces emotionally, so a face that shows no emotion looks negative to them.

Talking with Wags and Woofs

How can we see what's going on in a dog's mind and heart? We can tell a lot about how a dog is feeling from her body language.

Is her tail up and wagging more toward your left when you stand in front of her? The dog is probably feeling friendly.

If the hair on her shoulders is raised and her tail is wagging more toward your right, the dog may be feeling aggressive.

Are her head and tail down and her ears flattened? She's feeling insecure or scared.

Dogs' barks also reveal their feelings. Dogs do a lot of barking, sometimes way too much for humans within hearing range! Wolves, on the other hand, rarely bark.

Some scientists think that **barking** has become **a way for dogs** to express their feelings and needs to their **human companions**—and to each other.

Researchers Dr. Ádám Miklósi, Dr. Péter Pongrácz, and their team, working in Hungary, have shown that people can understand the meaning of different dog barks. The scientists played recordings of dogs barking under different circumstances and asked people what the dog was feeling. The listeners could tell if the dog was welcoming someone arriving, feeling alone and fearful, being playful, or warning away a threat. Even people who didn't own dogs could figure out what was on the dog's mind.

Dr. Andics's study showed that hearing "Good dog!" lights up both sides of your dog's brain and feels like the sweetest reward of all!

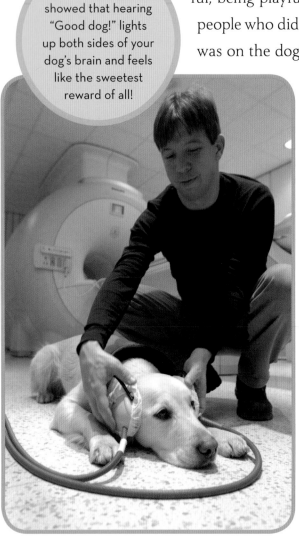

Dr. Attila Andics and his colleagues used an MRI machine in the laboratory to show that dogs can recognize emotions in people's voices. Their research shows that dogs process the *tone* of human speech—enthusiastic, neutral, or negative—in one part of the brain, while the *actual meaning* of the words is processed in a different brain region—just like human brains do. And when positive words are spoken in a positive tone, such as "Good dog!" the reward center lights up, just as it does when the dog gets a treat.

Doggy Jealousy

If you have a dog, you may have had this experience. You're walking your dog and someone else comes along with a really cute puppy. You stop to pet the puppy and, before you know it, your dog has flipped up your arm with his muzzle so that your hand lands on his head instead. So much for showing attention to another dog!

"Look at me, not her!"

Dr. Christine Harris and student Caroline Prouvost at the University of California, San Diego, experimented to learn if dogs feel jealousy. They found that dogs would act in a jealous fashion if their person pet a realistic stuffed dog that barked and whined. The dog would come over and push away the stuffed dog. But the dog was more likely to ignore attention his person gave to other items that were not doglike, such as a jack-o'-lantern pail. This research supports the idea that dogs don't want to share human attention with other dogs. *Pet me—don't pet him!*

Doggy Smarts

How smart are dogs? Turns out they're more intelligent than a lot of people think! For example, they have a sense of quantity. If someone secretly takes away a treat from a bunch of four or five she's seen, the dog acts confused—*where did that other one go?* This is just the way a human toddler reacts.

In general, dogs can understand about 165 words and gestures, and a really smart dog can remember more.

All in all, **scientists say** that an **average dog** is about as **smart** as a **two-year-old child.**

Chaser: One Very Smart Dog

Do you think your dog is smart? Wait until you meet Chaser. Retired psychology professor John Pilley believed that dogs are very smart, and he decided to prove it when he got a border collie puppy he named Chaser. Chaser learned the names of different objects. She was always petted and praised when she understood a name or a command. For years, Dr. Pilley kept buying and naming toys, first dozens of toys, then hundreds of toys, and now over a thousand toys! Bins full of all sorts of stuffed animals, balls, and dolls. Each one

has been given a unique name, and even if the floor is covered with her toys, Chaser can pick out any one by name when asked. Compare that to a human toddler, who knows around three hundred words.

And there's more. She also understands the difference between "Take doll to ball" and "Take ball to doll." She can pick out a named object just by seeing a picture of it. And if you sneak a new object into the group of toys and give it a name she's never heard, she'll find the strange object and bring it. Now that's a smart dog!

Part Three:
Sharing Our Lives

In the past, dogs and people often spent the day working together side by side. Now most people go off to work at jobs that don't include their dogs. But dogs are still considered an important part of our families, and they're more popular than ever. In the United States, four out of every ten households have at least one dog as part of the family, with more than 70 million dogs in the United States alone. We've also come to understand more about how interacting with dogs is helpful to people in a number of ways. Put these two things together, and it means that the lives of dogs and people have changed a lot in recent years.

Work Buddies

Carol runs Lucky Dog Day Camp in Kalispell, Montana, providing a happy place for dogs while their people are at work. Caring for as many as fifty dogs some days, Carol has her hands full. Luckily, she's "hired" Cypress, her big puffy white dog, to ride herd on the other canines and keep them in line.

When it's treat time, Cypress waits with her buddies.

Renee at 2 Barking Sisters' Dog Spaw in Missoula, Montana, works hard to keep dogs and their people happy, selling dog treats that look like delicious cookies and giving doggy baths and trims. Now that dogs are treated like treasured family members, their people like to find ways to pamper them.

Mara, a Karelian bear dog, helps out at the Spaw by putting the dogs and their people at ease.

"How may I help you?"

Feeling Good Together

Trained therapy dogs enjoy making people feel good. They visit retirement communities and hospitals to make new friends. They also go to libraries to keep children company while they read. Kids love reading to the dogs. Dogs don't correct them like a teacher or a parent might, and they don't interrupt. And when the children pet the dogs, it helps relieve any stress they might be feeling about reading aloud.

It's a **win-win** situation—the **dogs enjoy** the **attention,** and the **children enjoy** the **reading.**

"Good girl, Greta!"

Sometimes helping goes both ways. Kate has a special relationship with her dog, Greta. When Kate met Greta, it was love at first sight for them both. But as time went on, Kate could see that something wasn't quite right. It turned out Greta was almost completely deaf and could only hear low, rumbling sounds.

So Kate developed her own sign language for come, sit, stay, down stay, shake, no, and an enthusiastic thumbs-up for "Good girl!" Kate has become Greta's ears, and together they have formed a perfect partnership.

Helping Us Feel Safe

New understanding about the calming effect that dogs have on people and the love people and dogs share has led to a different kind of dog-human partnership—the emotional support dog.

Drew's puggle sticks to him—like glue—and makes him feel less anxious.

Glue is a friend magnet.

Glue, a puggle (a cross between a pug and a beagle), helps college student Drew cope with his anxiety and depression. Drew explains, "Before I got Glue, I had trouble keeping a schedule that allowed me to handle day-to-day activities without having panic attacks. Now Glue helps me keep to a schedule so my days run smoothly." He also had trouble sleeping before Glue came along.

Enjoying Our Best Friends

The most important job dogs have in their people's lives is just to be their best friends. And like best friends everywhere, people and dogs love having fun together. Towns have dog parks where dogs can run free, and oceanside communities have leash-free beaches where everyone can play in the water. People find other ways of enjoying time with their pets—dressing them up for parades, playing ball together, and sharing favorite free-time activities. Our dogs love it, and so do we.

As we understand more and more about how similar dogs and people are in their brains and body chemistry, we realize that we are truly meant for each other.

As **Dr. Gregory Berns** puts it, "**Dogs** are **people,** too."

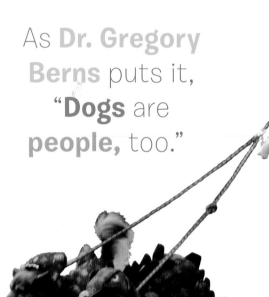

Resources for Young Readers

Books

Baines, Becky. *Everything Dogs: All the Canine Facts, Photos, and Fun You Can Get Your Paws On!* with Gary Weitzman. National Geographic Kids Everything. Washington, D.C.: National Geographic Children's Books, 2012.

Crisp, Marty. *Everything Dog: What Kids Really Want to Know About Dogs.* Kids' FAQs. Chanhassen, MN: NorthWord Press, 2003.

Horowitz, Alexandra. *Inside of a Dog—Young Readers Edition.* New York: Simon & Schuster, 2016.

Newman, Aline Alexander, and Gary Weitzman. *How to Speak Dog: A Guide to Decoding Dog Language.* Washington, D.C.: National Geographic Children's Books, 2013.

Websites

akc.org

This is the site for the American Kennel Club. You can learn basic information about the many breeds of dogs in the United States.

animalplanet.com/breed-selector/dog-breeds.html

> The Animal Planet website contains videos and information about specific dog breeds and dog behavior.

dognition.com

> This site gives you an opportunity to check out the unique profile of your own dog and, for a small fee, see what kind of personality traits he or she has. The site is operated by Dr. Brian Hare and other scientists who know a lot about dog behavior. You can browse the site for free.

Videos

The Atlantic, "The Origin of Dogs"
> theatlantic.com/video/index/499340/the-origin-of-dogs

Dr. Gregory Berns, "How Dogs Love Us"
> youtube.com/watch?v=eVw1zs2X3iA

Anderson Cooper, "Does Your Dog Really Love You?"
> cbsnews.com/news/anderson-cooper-does-your-dog-really-love-you/

Anderson Cooper, "How Dogs Express Their Emotions"
> cbs.com/shows/60_minutes/video/gelxt1VUC8XxN8zJ35dlqIVnAx3EkGVs/how-dogs-express-their-emotions

Anderson Cooper, "The Smartest Dog in the World"
> cbsnews.com/news/the-smartest-dog-in-the-world

Family Dog Project, various videos
> facebook.com/FamilyDogProject/videos/?ref=page_internal

Dr. Brian Hare, "Are Certain Breeds More Intelligent?"
> cbsnews.com/videos/are-certain-breeds-more-intelligent/

Source Notes

A sampling of resources consulted for this book

Part One: A Perfect Partnership

Ideas on how and where dogs originated:

Augliere, Bethany. "Ancient Genomes Suggest Dual Origin for Modern Dogs." *Nature*, June 2, 2016. nature.com/news/ancient-genomes-suggest-dual-origin-for-modern-dogs-1.20027.

Skoglund, Pontus, Erik Ersmark, Eleftheria Palkopoulou, and Love Dalén. "Ancient Wolf Genome Reveals an Early Divergence of Domestic Dog Ancestors and Admixture into High-Latitude Breeds." *Current Biology* 25, no. 11 (June 2015): 1,515–1,519. cell.com/current-biology/fulltext/S0960-9822(15)00432-7.

Zimmer, Carl. "Wolf to Dog: Scientists Agree on How, but Not Where." *The New York Times,* November 14, 2013. nytimes.com/2013/11/14/science/wolf-to-dog-scientists-agree-on-how-but-not-where.html.

Evidence about how long humans and dogs have been together:

Ensminger, John. "Canine Domestication May Have Begun 30,000 or More Years Ago." *Dog Law Reporter* (blog), February 1, 2013. doglawreporter.blogspot.com/search?q= Canine+Domestication+May+have+begun.

Dogs in rock art:

Harrigan, Peter. "Art Rocks in Saudi Arabia." *Aramco World* 53, no. 2 (March/April 2002): 36–47. aramcoworld.com/issue/200202/art.rocks.in.saudi.arabia.htm.

Dogs and people as possible hunting partners:

Frick-Wright, Peter. "Underdog." *Sierra,* January/February 2015. sierraclub.org/sierra/2015-1-january-february/feature/underdog.

Pointing:

Hare, Brian, and Vanessa Woods. *The Genius of Dogs: How Dogs Are Smarter Than You Think.* New York: Dutton, 2013.

Breeding of foxes not afraid of people:

Trut, Lyudmila. "Early Canid Domestication: The Farm-Fox Experiment." *American Scientist.* americanscientist.org/issues/id.813,y.0,no.,content.true,page.2,css.print/issue.aspx.

Herding dogs:

Victoria Werner, in discussion with the author, October 2014.

Part Two: The Science of Love

Editorial about science and emotions in dogs:

Berns, Gregory. "Dogs Are People, Too." *The New York Times,* October 5, 2013. nytimes.com/2013/10/06/opinion/sunday/dogs-are-people-too.html.

MRI research:

Berns, Gregory. *How Dogs Love Us: A Neuroscientist and His Adopted Dog Decode the Canine Brain.* Boston: Houghton Mifflin Harcourt, 2013.

Effects of dog petting on hormones in dogs and humans:

Odendaal, J. S., and R. A. Meintjes. "Neurophysiological correlates of affiliative behaviour between humans and dogs." *Vet J.* 165, no. 3 (May 2003): 296–301. ncbi.nlm.nih.gov /pubmed/12672376.

Dogs recognize differences between happy and angry human faces:

Lee, Jane J. "Dogs Know What That Smile on Your Face Means." *National Geographic,* February 12, 2015. news.nationalgeographic.com/news/2015/02/150212-dogs-human-emotion-happy-angry-animals-science/.

Müller, Corsin A., Kira Schmitt, Anjuli L. A. Barber, and Ludwig Huber. "Dogs Can Discriminate Emotional Expressions of Human Faces." *Current Biology* 25, no. 5 (March 2, 2015): 601–605. cell.com/current-biology/abstract/S0960-9822(14)01693-5.

Articles on meaning of dog barks:

Lewis, Susan K. "The Meaning of Dog Barks." *NOVA,* October 28, 2010. pbs.org/wgbh /nova/nature/meaning-dog-barks.html.

Owano, Nancy. "Budapest Team Studies How Humans Interpret Dog Barks." Phys.org, January 9, 2014. phys.org/news/2014-01-budapest-team-humans-dog-barks.html.

Pajer, Nicole. "What Your Dog's Barking Means." Cesar's Way. cesarsway.com/dog-behavior /barking-and-howling/what-is-your-dog-feeling-by-their-bark.

Dogs might recognize different emotions in human voices:

Andics, Attila, Márta Gácsi, Tamás Faragó, Anna Kis, and Ádám Miklósi. "Voice-Sensitive Regions in the Dog and Human Brain Are Revealed by Comparative fMRI." *Current Biology* 24, no. 5 (March 3, 2014): 574–578. cell.com/current-biology/abstract/S0960-9822(14)00123-7?_returnURL=http%3A%2F%2Flinkinghub.elsevier.com%2Fretrieve %2Fpii%2FS0960982214001237%3Fshowall%3Dtrue.

Hamers, Laurel. "Dog Brains Divide Language Tasks." *Science News* 190, no. 7 (October 1, 2016): 11. sciencenews.org/article/dog-brains-divide-language-tasks-much-humans-do.

Stromberg, Joseph. "Your Dog Can Tell from Your Voice if You're Happy or Sad." Smithsonian.com, February 20, 2014. smithsonianmag.com/science-nature/your-dog-can-tell-from-your-voice-if-youre-happy-or-sad-180949807/.

Meaning of dog barks:

Pongrácz, Péter, Csaba Molnár, Ádám Miklósi, and Vilmos Csányi. "Human Listeners Are Able to Classify Dog *(Canis familiaris)* Barks Recorded in Different Situations." *Journal of Comparative Psychology* 119, no. 2 (2005): 136–144. academia.edu/1542221/Human _Listeners_Are_Able_to_Classify_Dog_Canis_familiaris_Barks_Recorded_in_Different _Situations.

Jealousy in dogs:

Gorman, James. "Inside Man's Best Friend, Study Says, May Lurk a Green-Eyed Monster." *The New York Times,* July 23, 2014. nytimes.com/2014/07/24/science/entering-gray-area-study-says-dogs-can-be-green-with-envy.html.

Kiderra, Inga. "Dog Jealousy: Study Suggests Primordial Origins for the 'Green-Eyed Monster.'" UC San Diego News Center, July 23, 2014. ucsdnews.ucsd.edu/pressrelease /dog_jealousy_study_suggests_primordial_origins_for_the_green_eyed_monster.

Chaser:

Pilley, John W. *Chaser: Unlocking the Genius of the Dog Who Knows a Thousand Words,* with Hilary Hinzmann. Boston: Houghton Mifflin Harcourt, 2013.

Part Three: Sharing Our Lives

Lucky Dog Day Camp:

Carol Thill, in discussion with William Muñoz, November 2014.

2 Barking Sisters' Dog Spaw:

Renee Van Camp, in discussion with the author, November 2014, and William Muñoz, December 2014.

Therapy dogs:

Drew Estep, in discussion with the author, July 2014, and email messages to author, March 2015; in discussion with William Muñoz, October 2014.

Jasmine Bloemke, in discussion with William Muñoz, September 2014.

Kate McDermott, in discussion with the author, October 2014, and email messages to author, October 2014 and January 2015; in discussion with William Muñoz, October 2014.

Additional Sources

The following sources have been particularly useful in presenting key concepts in this book.

Books

Berns, Gregory. *How Dogs Love Us: A Neuroscientist and His Adopted Dog Decode the Canine Brain*. Boston: Houghton Mifflin Harcourt, 2013.

Hare, Brian, and Vanessa Woods. *The Genius of Dogs: How Dogs Are Smarter Than You Think*. New York: Dutton, 2013.

Horowitz, Alexandra. *Inside of a Dog: What Dogs See, Smell, and Know*. New York: Scribner, 2009.

Pilley, John W. *Chaser: Unlocking the Genius of the Dog Who Knows a Thousand Words*, with Hilary Hinzmann. Boston: Houghton Mifflin Harcourt, 2013.

Interviews

Dr. Attila Andics, research fellow, Family Dog Project, Eötvös Loránd University, Budapest, Hungary

Dr. Gregory Berns, distinguished professor of neuroeconomics and director of the Center for Neuropolicy and Facility for Education and Research in Neuroscience, and professor of psychology, Emory University, Atlanta

Lars Bjurström, photographer

Dr. Ludwig Huber, professor and head of Messerli Research Institute, University of Veterinary Medicine, Vienna, Austria

Dr. Ádám Miklósi, professor and head of Department of Ethology, Eötvös Loránd University, Budapest, Hungary

Dr. Daniel Mills, professor of veterinary behavioral medicine, School of Life Sciences, College of Science, University of Lincoln, Lincoln, UK

Photo Credits

Key: t—top, b—bottom, c—center, l—left, r—right, tl—top left, tr—top right, bl—bottom left, br—bottom right

pp. 2–3, 62–63, bimka/Shutterstock; **p. 4,** Julia Pleskachevskaia/Shutterstock; **p. 8,** correct pictures/Shutterstock (tl), Ariel Skelley/Getty Images (tr), William Muñoz (c), Tropical studio/Shutterstock (bl), ESB Professional/Shutterstock (br); **p. 9,** Tomsickova Tatyana/Shutterstock; **p. 10,** Jim Mann Taylor; **p. 11,** Lars Bjurström; **p. 12,** William Muñoz; **p. 13,** wizdata/Shutterstock; **pp. 14–15,** Dennis W Donohue/Shutterstock; **pp. 16–17,** William Muñoz; **p. 18,** Bruno De Faveri/Shutterstock (tl), Jim Cumming/Shutterstock (tr); **pp. 18–19,** Dora Zett/Shutterstock (b); **p. 19,** Alexandr Junek Imaging/Shutterstock (t); **p. 20,** Copyright © 2009 D. L. Anderson; **p. 21,** Phovoir/Shutterstock; **p. 22,** SPUTNIK/Alamy; **p. 23,** Amy Bassett/JAB Canid Education and Conservation Center; **p. 24,** Eric Isselee/Shutterstock (row 1 left, row 2 center, row 4 left, row 5 center, row 6 all, row 7 left and center), Kuznetsov Alexey/Shutterstock (row 1 center), gbarinov/Shutterstock (row 1 right), Man_Wanted_Media/Shutterstock (row 2 left), Gelpi/Shutterstock (row 2 right), Africa Studio/Shutterstock (row 3 left), Jagodka/Shutterstock (row 3 center), VitCOM Photo/Shutterstock (row 3 right), MilsiArt/Shutterstock (row 4 center), Csanad Kiss/Shutterstock (row 4 right), Adya/Shutterstock (row 5 left), MirasWonderland/Shutterstock (row 5 right), Max Topchii/Shutterstock (row 7 right); **p. 25,** U.S. Army photo by Sgt. Michael Needham, 102nd Mobile Public Affairs Detachment (l), U.S. Air Force photo by Sgt. Jeremy Bowcock/Flickr Creative Commons (r); **pp. 26–27,** Elizabeth W. Kearley/Getty Images; **p. 28,** iStock/406_Montanan; **p. 29,** Steve Oehlenschlager/Shutterstock (t), Best dog photo/Shutterstock (b); **p. 30,** HTeam/Shutterstock (tl), Nina Buday/Shutterstock (tr), Kiselev Andrey Valerevich/Shutterstock (c), siriwat sriphojaroen/Shutterstock (bl), Sergey Lavrentev/Shutterstock (br); **p. 31,** iStock/Kosamtu; **pp. 32–33,** Dr. Gregory Berns; **p. 34,** Monkey Business Images/Shutterstock; **p. 35,** bernatets photo/Shutterstock (t), vvvita/Shutterstock (b); **p. 36,** Dorothy Hinshaw Patent; **p. 37,** Dr. Daniel Mill (t), iStock/dhotard; **p. 38,** William Muñoz; **p. 39,** Crystal Alba/Shutterstock (l), alexei_tm/Shutterstock (r); **p. 40,** Eniko Kubinyi; **p. 41,** William Muñoz; **p. 43,** Chris Bott; **p. 44,** fizkes/Shutterstock (tl), Secheltgirl/Shutterstock (tr), goodluz/Shutterstock (c), conrado/Shutterstock (bl), Kamila Starzycka/Shutterstock (br); **pp. 45–47,** William Muñoz; **p. 48,** Lorraine Kourafas/Shutterstock; **pp. 49–52,** William Muñoz; **p. 53,** William Muñoz (tl, tr), bonzodog/Shutterstock (c), Christian Mueller/Shutterstock (b); **p. 54,** WitthayaP/Shutterstock.

Index